The Entrepreneur Millionaire Mindset

Master The Success Habits, Principles & Secrets To Unlock Your Millionaire Mind And Develop More Wealth, Money, Motivation, Focus, Abundance & Confidence

Jeffy Cooks

Table of Contents

CHAPTER 1

WHY ANYONE CAN MAKE MONEY ONLINE & HOW YOU CAN GET STARTED

As you're most likely already aware as you've came across this article – there are a plethora of ways to earn money online out there.

…So can you make money online – the answer is yes!!

So why doesn't everybody just quit their day jobs and take to the internet?

Well, unfortunately for many of us, self-doubt has taken over the decision-making computers that are our brains and decided for us that we simply 'can't do this' and 'can't do that', hindering our ability to ever even try.

CAN YOU MAKE MONEY ONLINE? OF COURSE! HERE'S A FEW EXAMPLES

Blogs, YouTube videos, affiliate marketing, retail arbitrage – these are just 4 of thousands of money-making opportunities out there that just about anybody can do. Yes, that includes **you**.

Regardless of whether or not you're a skilled wordsmith, an adept in web design or a master of Photoshop, working from home, thanks to the invaluable advancements of modern technology, has never been easier. Seriously, working from home is easier now than it ever has been in the past which is exactly why you should not doubt your skills to do so.

Many jobs that can be completed online require a little common sense and basic computer skills – nothing more. Being able to string together nicely-structured, fairly intelligent-sounding sentences, having decent conversational skills and, above all, the motivation to succeed can get you incredibly far in the online world.

So long as you have a computer, internet connection and the capacity to work independently, free from other workers you most certainly have the ability to work online.

BUT HOW CAN YOU MAKE MONEY ONLINE? HERE'S HOW TO GET STARTED

There are an absolute tonne of ways to earn money online out there – literally thousands. But how should you go about choosing the right and most profitable ones that work for you?

Well, to begin with, let's look at a three of the most popular and flexible ways.

- Affiliate marketing. Affiliate marketing is an incredibly powerful and flexible tool when it comes to establishing a steady, automated flow of income through the internet. Thousands and thousands of companies out there (Amazon, Nike, Adidas – you name it!) have affiliate programs available for anybody to sign up to. Once you sign up, the respective company will send you some links to products that are relevant to your niche. Then, you simply drop these links across your page, whether it be a social media account, blog, website or YouTube channel and get paid commission every single time a person clicks on it! The great thing about affiliate marketing is it has no strict requirements and so you can run an affiliate business through any platform you choose.

- Upwork.com Many freelance workers use the popular job-finding site Upwork. Upwork allows employers to post job opportunities to their pages that can be searched for depending on the needs of each worker. You may advertise yourself as a graphic designer, a content writer or a web-creator. Once you're setup, you can apply for whichever jobs suit you best and, if you succeed in your application, be paid to work online. I personally have taken on many positions through Upwork and have been working in coffee shops and sofas on my laptop for around a year now.

- Photography. Don't scroll down. In today's world the idea that you need to be an expert cameraman with top-of-the-range equipment to succeed in the photography is entirely false. Thanks to the building of sites such as Shuttershock, virtually anybody can earn money through photography. Even if you don't have the best camera in the world, simply taking photos that are likely to be highly demanded by companies looking to add images to their site will earn you decent money. Shuttershock requires users to pay membership fees monthly which they then use to pay individuals/businesses that provide the images. You'll be paid every single time a person downloads your image. The beauty of photography is that it can be done almost entirely passively. Once your photos are up, you'll receive payments for as long as they continue to be downloaded.

I have purposely picked out what I consider to be the most widely accessible and skill-less ways to earn money online, however there are many, many more.

The beauty of these three techniques are that none require any expert knowledge or qualifications yet can generate enough income to allow you to work entirely from home.

All are also incredibly flexible and can be tweaked to suit an individual's personal expertise. Affiliate marketing can be done through social media, websites, blogs and many more online platforms. Blogging can even also come in the form of 'vlogging'/video blogging – so even if you lack writing skills then you can deliver information in the form of video.

Upwork offers endless job opportunities that are updated with new posts virtually by the minute so there's bound to be a position there that's just right for you. Photography can also cover a wide range of areas. Photos can be taken of literally anything you have access to and, if you'd prefer to work entirely through the web, software like Photoshop can be used to create digital imagery to sell on/templates.

So, reverting back to the original question, can you make money online?

…Absolutely!

So Can You Make Money Online Easily?

The internet is the most diverse, interconnected, opportunistic resource around that can be harvested by just about anybody with access to it.

If total geographical freedom and cutting loose the chains that hold you to your current 9-5 job sounds right for you then don't wait any longer.

So now that you don't need to ask can you make money online – because the answer is obviously YES! Now just find what suits you, do your research and pursue the career path you've always wanted.

CHAPTER 2.

HOW TO OVERCOME & BUILD YOUR PERSISTENCE.

"**I** Can't Make Money" Is A Fear That Everyone Has Faced At One Time Or Another.

I'd tried making money online for years before I made any decent money.

I went through every single emotion…

I tried.

I failed.

I f**ked up completely.

I got bored.

I was distracted.

'I can't make money online' was a fear I faced almost everyday.

And eventually I gave up on a TON of my online business ventures.

But the biggest problem is just that…giving up. And giving up way too early…

YOU HAVE TO CONQUER YOUR FEAR.

If you give up too soon, you won't reap the rewards of your hard work.

The concept of making money online is beautiful.

BUT…

The reality is an insane amount of hard work.

And when most people realise just how much hard work it takes, they give up far too early.

Especially when starting a business comes with no guarantees.

And that's exactly why most people can't make money online.

It's a hard, frustrating game that demands an incredible amount of patience.

THE DREAM VS THE REALITY.

One of the reasons why people think they can't make money is that the dream is extremely different from the reality.

Being an entrepreneur is an incredible concept. BUT it takes a hell of a lot of hard work upfront…

For example:

All those digital nomads you see on Instagram, posting pics of their office on the beach. (yea that happens)

In reality, they work like dogs.

They're seriously motivated. They spend everyday focusing on that dream. And they're incredibly hard working.

Most digital nomads I've met are earning less than $1,000 a month…

…Some of them had been working for years & still earning pennies.

And that's really not unusual.

I don't pity them. I don't mock them. I don't doubt that one day they'll be crushing it.

Because success doesn't happen overnight.

It takes years & years of hard work.

Sure, there are exceptions – but in the majority of cases, it takes a long time to earn decent money.

And unfortunately, most people don't have that kind of determination.

They would't be able to handle the stress of the job.

And in end, they get so frustrated they give up.

If you can't make money online yet, and you're not willing to make sacrifices, you may never be happy as an internet marketer.

Because to become successful at working online, you need to be prepared to deal with some seriously testing situations.

Picture these moments for example:

- Not knowing how much money you're going to make all year.

- Not even knowing whether you'll make a dollar at all.

- Seeing your best friends earning at least 2X, 3X or 10X the amount of money you do.

- Facing the fear that you 'can't make money online' whilst dedicating every minute of every day to your online business.

- Dealing with some really crappy customers 24/7.

- Never taking a day off. (Seriously, I can't remember the last time I took a day off.)

- No pension or retirement fund until you start making decent money online.

…And that's just a few of the problems you'll face on a weekly basis.

WORRIED YOU CAN'T MAKE MONEY ONLINE? SHINY OBJECT SYNDROME IS YOUR BIGGEST ENEMY…

Most people can't make money online because they don't have the determination:

They don't want to spend 5 years of their life working towards something that pays very little reward in the meantime.

…And this whole vicious cycle leads to shiny object syndrome.

Here's how Shiny Object Syndrome is plaguing the internet marketing world:

1. You worry you can't make money online with your current idea.

2. So you look at other internet marketers who boast of the 'easiest, fastest & most hassle-free' way to make money online.

3. You jump onto a new idea & abandon the old business that you invested months of time, hard work & money into.

4. Then you realise that the new idea isn't perfect either – so the vicious cycle starts all over again!

Distraction is a HUGE issue – and it's incredibly seductive.

Because whether we realise it or not, we're always looking for an excuse to explain why we can't do something.

That way if we fail, we can blame it on something else.

It relieves your fear.

So if you find yourself looking for the next shiny object that will 'make you a million dollars in 24 hours',

STOP!

Because it's total F**KING BS!

And instead, keep grinding on your current project.

MAKING MONEY ONLINE IS ALL ABOUT YOUR MINDSET.

Making money online is all about how you motivated, determined & focused you are.

It's basically your whole mindset.

And if you haven't got the right mindset, you can't make money online.

Because your poor mindset will lead you into a trap:

- You'll bounce one from idea to the other, without sticking to your guns.

- You'll blame your failures on someone else.

- You'll be stuck in a vicious cycle of shiny object syndrome.

- You'll lack the motivation you need to succeed in this game.

Just remember this:

You've got an abundance of time. You can't rush success. You just have to see it through & keep going.

Work hard. Grind. Hustle…And stop trying to get everything overnight!

Thousands Of Internet Marketers Believe Life Is Always Greener On The Other Side…But There's No Golden Ticket.

HOW TO STOP FEELING LIKE YOU CAN'T MAKE MORE MONEY.

If you want to get good at something, you have to persevere.

It's the same if you're playing football, learning chess or becoming a doctor.

You're building a skill set, one that takes years to master.

And no one else can do it for you.

No coach.

No guru.

No fancy course that's giving you unrealistic expectations.

Sure, you might make money in the short-term but internet marketing is a long term game.

And you have your whole life to make money online.

Now there are some exceptions:

I have a few friends who made six figures within their first year. And that's awesome! But if it doesn't work out for you, don't lose hope!

In fact, the people I've met who made six figures online are still working like dogs.

They have so much drive & love for what they do that they're working even harder now to reach a million dollars online.

But that's the sort of mindset that will make you successful!

Just remember that you have an abundance of time.

There's no rush – especially if you're enjoying the journey.

And with so much time on your hands, you can afford to work at a steady pace whilst staying focused.

So change your mindset. Be prepared to persevere. And stay 100% focused.

That's all it takes.

CHAPTER 3.

WHY YOU SHOULD NEVER GIVE UP.

1. YOU CAN'T FAIL IF YOU DON'T GIVE UP.

What would you do if you were absolutely certain you would succeed?

Whether you want to make a decent side income or hustle online full time, it's impossible to fail if you don't give up.

The best things in life take time. All you need to do is invest it wisely.

But you have an abundance of time. And that's all that making money online will cost you.

Everything you need to make money online can be bought with your own time.

- You don't need to hire anyone else.

- You don't need to spend big on paid advertising.

- You don't need to pay for a fancy course or the latest book by a business guru.

And believe me, if working online was easy, everyone would be doing it!

To create a successful business online, all you need is time and hard work.

You can make money online without spending a

single cent – as you'll find out here!

That's the formula for making money online – don't be fooled by anything else!

You literally have the rest of your life ahead of you.

So what have you got to lose?

2. EVERY SUCCESSFUL PERSON HAS FACED THE SAME PROBLEMS AS YOU RIGHT NOW.

You've got to respect the process when it comes to achieving anything.

You're on a journey right now. And it's the same journey every successful person has travelled.

There will be loads of times when you want to give up.

In fact, I can almost guarantee this:

Every single online entrepreneur has thought 'should I give up on making money online?'

It's 100% natural. It's the journey to success.

And no one can take that journey for you – it's you and you alone.

Need proof?

Let's take a look at a few successful people who could've given up on BUT didn't:

- JK Rowling was rejected dozens of times, received

Government Aid and couldn't even afford a computer when she wrote the Harry Potter series.

- The Beatles, who sold over 250 million records, were told they had "no future in show business"!

- Albert Einstein couldn't speak until he was 4 years old. In his school report, his teachers claimed he'd never amount to anything.

- Walt Disney was fired for "not being creative enough" – he still holds the record for the most Oscars won by one person. On one of his earlier ventures he even went bankrupt.

…All of these people were told they weren't good enough.

…All of them could've easily quit.

…Yet all of them went on to be incredibly successful because they never gave up!

Failure is just one small step on the road to success. Don't let it fool you.

3. You'll Have Wasted Hours, Days, Months Or Even Years Of Hard Work.

You've done the hard work.

…Not it's time to reap the rewards.

Give up on making money now and you'll lose the hours, days and months of hard work you've put into working online.

There are tons of digital nomads I've met who were literally a stone's throw from making money online – yet they failed at the last hurdle.

They simply gave up, packed their bags and decided to head home.

So here's a few examples of where you could give up but need keep going:

- Dropshipping websites with no customers.

- Fiverr accounts that aren't generating enough sales (YET!).

- UpWork profiles with bad reviews.

…So many people experience the above and decide to give up on making money online.

But here's the thing:

These are all just challenges along the way. You don't need to give up!

Persist and you'll reap the rewards.

It just takes time.

4. YOU'LL BUILD HABITS FOR SUCCESS.

If you can learn how to launch your own business and never give up on making money online, you can apply that same experince to become successful in almost anything in your life!

Making money online. Gym. Hobbies. Sports. Losing

weight. Competing.

These are all examples of where persistence counts.

…And the list is endless.

So don't give up on making money online – because you're about to learn a skill that literally pays off for the rest of your life!

5. You Knew This Was Going To Be Tough.

Let's be 100% honest…

You knew that starting an online business was going to be seriously hard work.

And don't even try to tell me you believed all the get rich quick schemes!

If you've already made the choice to try and make money online, you knew just just how difficult it was going to be.

…You know that it requires endless hours of hard work, hustle and grinding.

In fact, that's what I love about this lifestyle!

You get to see the results of all of your hard work:

The sales, the customers, the website traffic grow exponentially as you continue to keep going.

Now let's contrast this to your other main lifestyle option…

Say you're working in a full time job for a corporate company.

No matter how hard you work…

No matter how many weekends you waste…

No matter how many hours you spend in meetings…

You can still end up facing a whole bunch of shitty situations that are out of your control.

Redundancy. Pay cuts. Ruthless colleagues.

These are all out of your control!

But if you work online for yourself, you can have almost complete control.

You'll benefit from all the hard work you put in.

You'll have complete job security as long you never give up on making money online – and that's the beauty of it!

Why give up control of your life to someone else?

6. SUCCESS COMES FROM FAILURE.

Failure is incredibly character building.

It makes you stronger. It makes you adapt. It makes you become more resilient.

And if you give up on making money now, you won't become stronger. You won't adapt. You won't become more resilient.

…You'll simply learn to quit when things get tough – and that will never help you!

All the traits to become successful grow from failure. You have to keep going or you won't grow as a person.

There's just one thing you need to do:

Learn from the mistakes you make.

Think of business like a game:

The more you practice, the better you'll get.

You have to hone your entrepreneurial skills and keep them sharpened.

And if you quit whilst everyone else persists, you'll lose the game by default.

You'll voluntarily give up everything you've worked for.

And you won't get the chance to grow as an entrepreneur.

So why give up on making money online now?

7. YOUR FUTURE SELF WILL THANK YOU.

…Seriously!

All the hard work you put in now is worth it.

Just imagine reminiscing in 5 years time and thinking back to the point that you decided not to give up on making money online…

That will be an amazing feeling!

…You'll look back and remember all the times you kept going.

..All the times you could've quit but didn't.

…All the times you thought about quitting but you didn't listen, you just kept going.

It's kind of like the marshmallow theory:

You can eat 1 marshmallow now or you can receive 2 marshmallows later.

In other words, make a small sacrifice of hard work now and you'll reap the benefits later.

This is all about self control. And it pays off, BIG time!

The truth is, if you master your mindset, you'll master your future success.

8. YOU HAVE TO GO BEYOND YOUR COMFORT ZONE TO GROW AS A PERSON.

Feeling frustrated?

Wanna give up on making money online all the freakin' time?

Well, that just shows you're leaving your comfort zone!

You gotta crack a few eggs to make an omelette right?

And that feeling of frustration you're getting is simply your mind and body growing as you become stronger.

It's like the gym:

You have to tear your muscle fibres for them to become stronger.

If you don't go out of your comfort zone, you won't become better at what you do.

It's the only way you'll learn!

So don't give up on making money online – because that rut you're stuck in is challenging you to break through your own barriers.

Break through now and you'll discover a whole new world of success on the other side…

9. THINK ABOUT THE REASONS YOU'VE GOT THIS FAR.

What made you start up your online business?

To never give up on making money online, you have to constantly refuel your motivation.

Your desire to succeed needs to be replenished at every opportunity.

For me, working online just made perfect sense. Here's why I got started:

- You can travel & work wherever you want in the world.

- You're constantly learning and growing.

- You reap the rewards of your hard work.

- It's a character building journey that's helps you become more resilient.

- As a digital nomad, you're surrounded by incredibly inspiring people who want to see you succeed.

- You get to avoid the office politics that comes with a full time job.

- You have far, far more freedom!

- You get to wake up in the morning whenever you want!

- …I mean, in what other job do you have the ability to work from home in your underwear whilst making money?

Casual Friday for the Telecommuter

On a serious note though:

To keep your motivation topped up, you need to understand exactly why you're doing this.

Otherwise you'll give up on making money online because you don't have any drive to achieve the end results.

So think about what motivates you:

…Write down your reasons.

…Keep them in a place where you can see them.

…And never forget the reasons behind why you're living this lifestyle.

10. IT AIN'T EASY BUT IT'S WORTH IT.

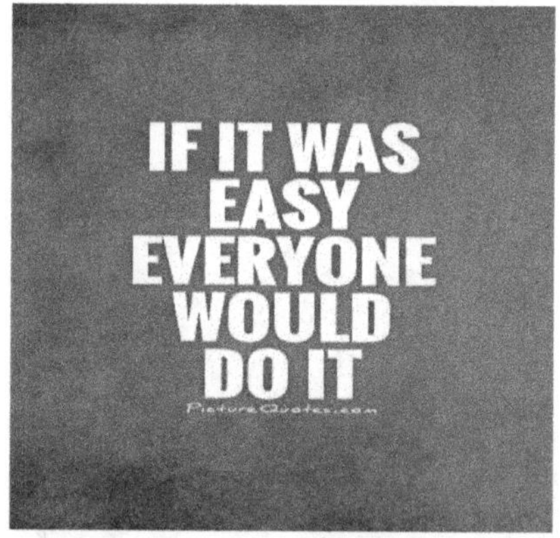

If this lifestyle was easy, everyone would be doing it!

But here's the brutal truth:

90% of businesses FAIL.

Not many people make in in business – online or offline. It's a psychological, draining game that most just aren't prepared to deal with.

They want the easy, simple life where they're told when, where and how to work.

But give up on making money online and you'll give up the rewards that come with it.

Because the concept of being successful online is easy.

Putting it into practice is hard.

If you're willing to work hard, you'll make it. You don't even need to spend much time on your online business – you just have to be consistent.

You have to persist – even when the chips are stacked against you.

THAT'S LITERALLY THE DIFFERENCE BETWEEN SUCCESS AND FAILURE!

CHAPTER 4.

10 POWERFUL REASONS TO QUIT YOUR JOB & START YOUR OWN BUSINESS.

Why on earth would you quit your perfectly stable, hard-earned position that pays your bills and keeps your food on the table? Because, thanks to the advancements of the modern age and computer technology, full-time jobs are simply no longer a necessity and more a routine held by the naive and unaware worker bees of today's world that are yet to discover the beauty of passive income.

Working when you want to, how you want to, being the boss of yourself and having total geographical freedom to travel with loved once is the incentive driving many millions of entrepreneurs into ditching their 9-5 for a life of freedom and wealthiness.

This article will explore 10 reasons to quit your job and begin earning online…

1. BECOME THE MASTER OF YOUR OWN FATE

This is one the best reasons to quit your job right now!

While, yes, full-time jobs may be considered 'secure' and 'stable' ways to earn money, this is a common misconception. Being a worker for your boss is most certainly not a stable way to generate an income.

Regardless of your position, higher up management executives have the power to cast you aside if they see it as being better for their company. Business is a dog-eat-dog world and, if you're considered not to be pulling your weight, managers can easily cut off your 'stable' stream of income and leave you drowning in the deep end.

Don't let this frighten you.

Let it entice you into spreading your roots wider and establishing multiple streams of income. There are a plethora of articles out there ready to educate you in the world of passive income (have a browse around our website and you'll find hundreds of ways to earn online). Read up, learn the facts and escape the slave trade dressed up as 'secure income'.

2. FREEDOM

Simply put, having a business that can be run from any device with internet connection is like being given keys to complete financial freedom.

Having a full-time job will tie you to a nearby location and force you stay there, threatening financial insecurity if you choose to move elsewhere. Abandoning your day job and setting up streams of online income is a great way to have freedom to travel and explore the world, spending your time doing things you actually want to and not working 24/7.

3. QUIT BEING A NUMBER

It's an unfortunate fact that many workers are treated like numbers – millions of tiny parts that make up a huge whole divided into employers and employees. Even those in high managerial positions are still very much employees with the exception of the CEO. Working for yourself allows you to break this pattern of being another cog in a machine.

4. FOLLOW YOUR PASSION

Countless people spend 70% of their lives in a job they simply don't care about. Society has created a fast-flowing conveyor belt on which people are firmly glued from the age of around four right up until retirement.

Go to school, get an education, get a degree, go to university and work hard to get your grades so that you can get a decent paying job. We've all heard it before and although some have, many don't question the system and follow instructions blindly without considering other options, being told that those that do go on to work independent of a full-time job are the exceptions. This is wrong, and an utter lie.

Break the shackles of society and do it your way – set up your own sources of passive income. Invest some time into getting them started and reap the benefits for a lifetime.

5. TECHNOLOGY WILL REPLACE YOU

The advancements of our modern technological world pose an unfortunate threat to many human-led careers. Like it or not, computers are replacing many job opportunities and will likely overpower much of our world in the coming years.

Whether it be self-checkout machines, automatically driven taxis or online accounting services, computer technology is advancing at a rapid rate and is encouraging business owners to ditch paying their workers and to invest in technology that does everything for them. Entrepreneurship, however, will not be replaced hence why you should get started with your business as soon as you can.

6. STARTING A BUSINESS HAS NEVER BEEN EASIER

Really, it hasn't.

There are so, so many different options out there for you to get started online. Dropshipping, retail arbitrage, affiliate marketing, stock investing, selling on Etsy, eBay, Amazon, blogging, writing eBooks – these are, believe it or not, a small handful of the ways in which you can start earning online.

Furthermore, starting a business has never been cheaper! Setting up a profitable, long-lasting business can now be done with as little as a few thousands pounds and, while this may seem steep, you can earn this in very little time with the internet alone.

7. DREAMS

Have you ever dreamt of having a full-time job that binds you to a city and won't let you leave without sacrificing your annual salary? Of course not.

This is slavery in disguise and we all need to open our

eyes to it. Don't let money be your master, take control and start living your dream now.

8. YOU FEEL LIKE YOU CAN'T DO ANYTHING ELSE

Your job is making you feel trapped and like you can never escape. This is a good enough reason as any to quit. You're a human, the most intelligent lifeform known to exist. Don't undermine your capabilities and settle for contentment – be the exception.

9. MONEY IS NOT THE KEY TO HAPPINESS.

Really, it isn't…And that's one of the most powerful reasons to quit your job & follow your passion.

Countless studies have shown that even the happiness lottery winners fizzles out after a few months or so. You may not become an instant millionaire after quitting your job but you can spend time with your children.

You can go out and spend time doing the things you life. You can go out for meals with your wife and spend your earnings on holidays. Slaving away at a day job for money is not worth it when you have options to do so much more with your time.

10. BECAUSE YOU CAN!

Simple. You can achieve your dream, so why wouldn't you?

CHAPTER 5.

10 EASY WAYS TO MAKE MONEY ONLINE.

With all information known to man at our fingertips and portable devices that allow us to tap into the web almost anywhere, there are a tonne of ways you can earn money online with very little effort.

This article teach you 10 easy ways to make money online…

10 EASY WAYS TO MAKE MONEY ONLINE:

1. **Matched Betting**. Don't panic — I'm not suggesting you blow all of your money on gambling in the hope of earning big. Believe it or not, this is a top pick for easy ways to make money online! Tonnes of betting agencies offer free bets when you bet using them (bet £20 and receive a free £20 bet, for example. By taking advantage of these free bets you can earn serious amounts of money for doing virtually nothing. Coral.co.uk are offering £20 worth of free bets for betting just £5 which is just one of a tonne of free-bet offers out there. Search around and make the most of these while you still can!

2. **Surveys**. A classic way of earning money online is through surveys. They require incredibly little effort and can be done from literally anywhere with wi-fi. The great thing about using online surveys is that you can do as many as you wish and whenever

you wish. You're not tied into doing a set amount per day/week and can simply just log in, power through a couple and get paid whenever you have a few moments to spare. Opinion Outpost and SurveyMonkey are the most reputable platforms for surveying. Just set up and account, put in your details and get going free of charge!

3. **Blogging**. Blogging is an excellent way not only to earn money online but to promote other business/products you already sell. A blog is simply just a website to which you post regular content, or 'blog posts', to your audience. You may decide to run a travel blog and post about where to go on holiday, perhaps you run a blog all about football and updates for your favourite teams – whatever it is make sure you choose a specialised niche to maximise your traffic. WordPress and Squarespace offer low prices for excellent website-creation tools to help you get started.

4. **Rewards cards.** Rewards cards are a super simple way of earning money for making no changes to your daily routine and simply doing exactly what you already do anyway. Rewards cards will award you points every time you spend money (Costa offer a card that gives you 10 points every time you spend £1, for example) that can be redeemed on a whole host of prizes – free hotel rooms, holidays, gift cards – the list is endless. Rewards cards such as the Sapphire Preferred Card will give you a free $500 if you spend $4,000 within 90 days. If you're

likely to spend this much anyway then you're essentially getting given free money!

5. **Selling**. Having a search around your attic (and wherever else you put unused items) to find items that could be sold is a super easy way to make money and free up some space in your house. Reselling old phones, clothes, whatever it is you can find will earn you a surprisingly high amount of cash. Sites such as Ebay and Gumtree are your best bet for reselling and offer fairly low listing fees too, maximising your profits and earning you more cash.

6. **Advertising**. Advertising can be done in a variety of forms – affiliate marketing, AdSense and direct-selling. Tonnes of companies offer affiliate market programs that you can sign up to simply by having a website. They'll email you affiliate links to put onto your site and, when people click on your site, you'll be paid commissions for the money earned by the company. AdSense is a scheme run by Google that allows you to choose ads that relate to your niche and, again, receive commission for each click made.

7. **Upwork & Fiverr.** Upwork and Fiverr are sites that allow employers to publish ads for jobs they have available. If you're skilled in writing, programming, website creation – practically anything then there's guaranteed to be a job opportunity out there for you. I've completed a

tonne of jobs through Upwork – all of which have been done entirely through my laptop. If you love the thought of freelancing and working in your pyjamas/in coffee shops, these websites are definitely for you.

8. **Create a course.** Using a website such as Udemy you can create your very own course to sell at a price. If you're particularly knowledgeable in a certain area then you most certainly can turn your knowledge into an unlimited source of passive income. Simply converting what you already know into a comprehensive guide hugely increase your monthly profits. Udemy even have a free course on how to create your first course!

9. **Ebooks**. Are you looking for easy ways to make money online passively? Writing an ebook can take as little as a few weeks and can earn you money for as long as you live. Simply browsing Amazon's Kindle store to see which books are selling most frequently at the moment and creating a book to match this demand is a super easy and relatively time-efficient way of earning. Check out our guide on how to write an ebook to get started!

10. **Website flipping**. Buying domain names, improving them and selling them at an increased price is another great way to earn some extra cash. It's one of the most popular picks for easy ways to make money online. Simply browse around for sites that are for sale that may have some potential

for adding value, drop in some affiliate links & AdSense campaigns, earn as much as you can from the site and sell it when it begins to run dry. It's really that simple.

35

CHAPTER 6.

HOW TO GET RICH FROM NOTHING.

We all want to earn more money. Whether it's to fund holidays, buy a new car, pay off a mortgage – increasing your annual income is a great way to relieve stress and do more with your time.

Unfortunately, many of us shy away from great opportunities to earn because we're scared to fail. Making investments into companies that could lose value and devoting time to writing a book that might not work out seems like an incredibly daunting task and one that few of us choose to go through with. However, living an entirely risk-free life is exactly what leaves many of us dissatisfied and unhappy with our current position.

Thankfully, not all methods of earning are incredibly risky and many are a lot easier than most of us think. You no longer have to be a stock-exchange expert or be born into royalty to become a millionaire.

This article will run you through some excellent, fool-proof ways that will teach you how to get rich from nothing…

GOALS

Before you embark on any journey you need to decide where you're going. It's no good just grabbing all the money from wherever you can if you're hoping to make some serious long-term cash.

First things first, you need to establish your goals. Where do you want to be in a year's time?

Perhaps you hope to double your monthly income before you hit your next age milestone. Maybe you want to have put away your first million by the time you're 65. Whatever your goal is, you need to stay committed to it.

Keep track of your monthly expenses and earnings and try to always keep a sensible gap between them. Save with the intention of being able to get by for the next couple of years if all of your current sources of income are cut off. If you spend £3,000 a month, try to keep at least £24,000 saved up in the bank.

This way, even if you do suffer some serious losses on your journey you'll always have some cash to fall back on.

HOW TO GET RICH FROM NOTHING: INVESTING

First and foremost, investing your savings is a sure way to allow you to build up your savings overtime.

You should aim to put away at least 10% of your monthly earnings into savings. Make sure you do not touch these savings – don't dip into them if you need a holiday or a new car or whatever it may be. These are your investment funds.

Take these funds and invest them into companies. Buying shares in companies will prevent your cash from gathering dust and will allow you to earn passively without having to actually do anything.

Investing through your bank or putting savings into a Roth IRA is a great way to generate passive income and will free up your time so that you can diversify your efforts and establish multiple streams of revenue.

Above investing in companies, you should always remember to invest in yourself. Spend the money you do have on improving your skills, learning about finances and increasing your worth as an individual, not just an entrepreneur.

HOW TO GET RICH FROM NOTHING: MAKE USE OF YOUR TALENTS

Even if they haven't yet discovered it yet, everybody is talented in one area or another. The area which you feel most passionate about is typically that which you're most knowledgeable in, therefore utilising your talents to earn you money is an excellent place to begin.

Perhaps you're particularly skilled in writing or playing a musical instrument. Using this talent as a launchpad for your financial journey will not only give you some valuable tools to begin with but will also ensure that the area of expertise you're pursuing is one that you actually care about.

How To Get Rich From Nothing: Establish Multiple Streams of Revenue

Many, many people make the mistake of relying solely on a single source of income. However, if ever this stream were to be cut off then most of us would have nothing to fall back on.

The entrepreneurs key to success is never to put all of their eggs in one basket – rather splitting their 'eggs', so to speak, amongst multiple baskets. Perhaps you already have a well paid position at your current workplace that earns you enough to get by. Rather than depending entirely on this single position to supply all of your financial needs, spread your earnings across a variety of independent sources.

This can be done in a variety of ways that don't have to involve increasing your weekly hours at another day job. Maybe you choose to set up an online business in the form of a blog, website or store. All three of these sources will earn you passive income that does not require you to actually 'go into' work every day. Once set up, these sources of income will provide a steady stream of income on their own.

Of course, building up multiple streams of income will take time to complete at first and you will be putting in a significant number of hours to begin with. However, once up and running these methods will supply you with constant cash for no more work at all – earning you far more than you would normally receive from a day job.

And there you have it – a handful of super easy tips to help you diversify your income and begin your journey towards getting rich in the next year. As always, stay consistent with your efforts and don't shy away from earning in the face of defeat. You may well suffer losses however just remember these are all part of your journey to financial freedom.

CHAPTER 7.

MONEY AFFIRMATIONS.

Many people have sufficient knowledge of how to make money yet they simply don't. There are a tonne of articles out there revolving around earning money, establishing multiple streams of revenue, stocks and trades, you name it, however people **still** settle for the norm. A 9-5, earned income lifestyle that ties its workers to one location and threatens them with financial turmoil if they dare to leave. So, if there exist ways to escape this norm, many of which you have likely already heard of before considering you've reached this article, *what on earth is holding everybody back?*

The answer – attitude. Success originates in the mind and lacking in the correct attitude is a guaranteed way to limit your financial growth. This article will explain exactly how you can adjust your perspective to attract wealth in all areas and persevere when streams run drier than usual.

MONEY AFFIRMATIONS: THE IMPORTANCE OF YOUR BRAIN...

Positive affirmations are simple, short statements that, when read repeatedly, help to reprogram your subconscious mind to integrate a particular belief. Your brain is a lot like a maze of winding paths. The more a walkway is utilized, the more downtrodden the grass that covers it will become and thus the more that path will be automatically used. Let me rephrase that a little more clearly – if walking in the woods, you are far more likely to follow pathways that have been used frequently rather than taking disused, overgrown routes. Your brain is a sea of intertwining pathways that work in this exact manner.

Every single brain is filled with trillions (yes, *trillions)* of tiny cells called 'neurons'. These neurons, when activated, send electrical signals that, in turn, cause some sort of change in your body. Your brain builds clusters of these neurons over time so that it can operate more efficiently. If you saw a dog, for example, you would not need to recall all of your past experiences with four legged creatures, identify its ears and snout and wait for it to bark to conclude that, yes, this animal is a dog. No, your brain instantly recognises this animal as a dog because it has a section of neurons dedicated to this knowledge. Clever.

Now, here's the key bit. These neuronal pathways act as great shortcuts to make things run more smoothly upstairs. However, the brain is, of course, a finite space that cannot house endless amounts of neurons. Therefore, when a pathway is not used, it is lost. Alternatively, and most importantly, if a pathway is used frequently then it becomes stronger. **Your brain will automatically use that pathway without you consciously having to choose to do so.**

…And Why This is Relevant

Now you may be wondering what on earth this information has to do with wealth and earning money.

Brains are naturally negative, pessimistic machines and are built this way to ensure our survival (more on this another time). Therefore, naturally, if you suffer from a financial loss, you will naturally wish to pull out of a project to prevent any further losses. Strengthening your neural pathways is absolutely key to building a positive attitude towards your financial journeys and, in turn, increasing your wealth. Positive affirmations are the perfect way to change your brain's natural assumptions and to switch your vision to focus on the positive rather than the negative. This process abandons pessimistic neural pathways and builds fresh, positive shortcuts for your brain to take. Through practice, you will no longer automatically think pessimistically and will begin to see things differently.

How to Use Money Affirmations

So what exactly *is* a positive affirmation?

An affirmation is a short, positive statement that you make to yourself frequently to rewire your subconscious brain. Examples may include, 'I am in control of my happiness' or 'I am wealthy'. It's best to formulate your own affirmations that are specific to your beliefs and goals. Focus on what you hope for and would like to achieve and base your affirmations on this. I would recommend aiming to have a list of around 3-5 affirmations tailored to your goals.

After building a bank of affirmations, write them down somewhere easily accessible – perhaps in a notebook or on your phone. You should aim to read through these affirmations around 2-3 times for 3 minutes, every single day for the next couple of months. I recommend reading them just before bed and right after waking up as your subconscious mind is most active during these times.

EXAMPLES OF MONEY AFFIRMATIONS

Although it's best to think of your own affirmations that suit you, below are a list of popular ones that you may choose if you wish.

- Money is good, I love money

- I am consciously happy and positive about money.

- Money is simply an energy that allows me freedom

- I attract money naturally to me. I am a money magnet

- I am not a slave to money. Money is attracted to me.

- I am wealthy and abundant.

CHAPTER 8.

HOW TO ATTRACT WEALTH - THE LAW OF ATTRACTION.

The focal point for those who have already had success in the Law of Attraction or those who are first timers looking to unravel more information about the Laws of Attraction are most likely "Money" and "Wealth."

Today's society has taught us from childhood, that the goal in life or "American Dream" is to be the richest by unlawful means or "Life or Death" sacrifices. Were you a child that often watched your parents struggle financially? Watching your parents live life payday to payday can be tough yet, effective on your adulthood.

Most parents often feel that they will never get out of debt, or be financially stable, so they teach that lifestyle to they're kids. It makes perfect sense!

Although, those going down a great path in life are dreaming for things such as: great health, great passion for their jobs or careers, Happy marriages, and let's not forget financial freedom. When your life is in order financially, you really get to think about what's important in life! Not only do you get to think about what you want out of life, but you can also live stress free and burden free. One thing to always keep in mind if you want wealth is to be a positive thinker and bring a "Take charge" attitude! Procrastinating never got anybody, anywhere.

Having a positive attitude is often the backbone to The Law of Attraction.

HOW TO ATTRACT WEALTH: THE LAW OF ATTRACTION

Author, Wallace D. Wattles, was one of the first to show a outstanding impact that The Law of Attraction can have on any financial situation. Wallace published a book called " The Science of Getting Rich" in 1910. In Wallace's book, he discussed how mental stability can effect financial wealth.

Other great author's who have shown or proven that The Law of Attraction can have a tremendous impact on all financial situations are Prentice Mulford. He was an author and humorist. He had a collage of essays on The Law of Attraction. These essays were called "Some Laws of Health and Beauty", "Good", and lastly "lll Effects of Thought." These were all written in 1891. Ralph Waldo Trine was an American author, lecturer and salesman. Ralph was also good friends with Henry Ford; they both enjoyed the discussion of success. Ralph published his book " In Tune with the Infinite " in 1897. Lastly, Thomas Troward was in my opinion, the most strongest influence and had the hardest impact on The New Thoughts Movement. He was English author who wrote an published 6 books in his lifetime. Although, the book that refers to the topic of The Law of Attraction is "The Law and the World" published in 1917.

One thing to know is that it's fairly hard to follow The

Laws of Attraction without it going unnoticed. People fail to realize that wealth isn't just about the money! Wealth can be gained in numerous ways such as: hard work, education, appearance and the list goes on. The key goal is to aim for peace, and positivity in your love life, health, and career. After you've got your personal life in order, you will be a magnet to financial success!

HOW TO ATTRACT WEALTH: DON'T BE A VICTIM!

Stop blaming everyone for your financial problems. The lifestyle you're currently living was not chosen for you. You have or had the same opportunity as the next rich guy, so start making plans and goals for yourself to accomplish. And let's actually accomplish them with no excuses or hesitations. Let your mind become overcrowded with thoughts of money. Get ecstatic when you come in contact with any bills and be grateful for the ones you have!

HOW TO ATTRACT WEALTH: CREATE MORE ABUNDANCE!

If you have a hard time getting in the money spirit, here are a few things you may be willing to try. Write abundance checks to yourself.

Once a month fill out a check with your name and a amount of your preference, etc. Then sign it under whatever name you wish! Not a real name, a silly name like "Fairly Godmother."

Next, try not to constantly get the needy feeling for money...

...Feeling needy will only create more financial problems for you in the long run. Next on the list is to be in a joyful or happy mood. Don't you often realize when you're happy, you become a magnet to great things? It's like you become lucky.

Then, change your pessimistic mindset to a positive one. When you say I "can't" afford it, you're really just worsening your chances for becoming able to afford it later. So start telling to yourself I "can" afford it! Lastly, For now on, when you see money lying around, grab it! That money was put in mid- air just for you. Or pretend the money found you! "Grab it, It's yours!"

How To Attract Wealth: Let It Flow To You

Money can be compared to a lot of things but I've never heard of it being compared to electricity! Although, money has it as ways of being just like electricity.

Many people blame money for their mistakes and are afraid to face their everyday responsibilities. Everything you want to manifest requires spirituality accordingly. Spirituality is an intense feeling as well as a healthy and balanced love for something, especially money. Keep pictures or symbols of money in your mind to keep you focused and to help remind yourself of why you even started what you did! Always remember, before you take action, think it through.

Your subconsiousness is to be put to the test when leading you to the right path of actions. Lastly imagine you would feel like if you were wealthy. Think about real numbers and commas, make it the main thought in your mind of how rich you want to be. If you have these thoughts regularly, do it at a time that works best with your schedule!

CHAPTER 9.

WHY YOU DON'T NEED MONEY TO MAKE MONEY.

Here's the truth – you don't need money to make money!

Many, many people are reluctant to create a business (or even *think* about creating a business) for fear of high investment costs. It's a common myth that starting a business requires money, however this just simply is not the case. This article will show you just how easy it is to start your very own entrepreneurial empire without having to sell a kidney to fund it.

WHY YOU DON'T NEED MONEY TO MAKE MONEY: TOOLS FOR CREATING A BUSINESS

- The right mindset. The key to any success is persistence and perseverance. You **must** be willing to invest your time if not your money – although businesses may generate their own passive income over time, you will need to put a fair amount of elbow grease to begin with. Hard work always pays off.

- Thinking in the long term. Thinking in years rather than days will massively boost your motivation and drive to keep going with your business. Although entrepreneurialism isn't a get-rich-quick scheme, it will, with time and effort, give you total freedom to travel the world and make the most of your time will still generating a full-time income.

- Supply and demand. Is your niche taking advantage of something which people will want and will pay for, or is it based solely on your personal interests rather than those of others? It is important to match the needs of the market and to fill a hole in the industry that is not currently being filled.

- Don't make excuses! Your excuses are your personal barriers – claiming that your business will not work because you have 'no time', 'no money', 'no good ideas' is a defeatist attitude that will only set you up for failure. Your beliefs about what will happen will massively influence the reality you create for yourself. For example, if you believe that you will 'never create a successful business' you will limit yourself with this mindset. If you truly do not believe you are able to create a successful business, you will likely put in far less effort into making this wish a reality and thus *will never create a successful business*. Believe in yourself. You are more than capable of achieving your dreams – your future self has already achieved them and is waiting for you to make the right decisions. Make them.

YOUR DREAM

Your future is your control – you seriously don't need money to make money. That is a fact. Everybody has a dream, somewhere, even if you haven't uncovered it yet.

That dream is your destiny, it is what you were put here to accomplish.

Do not let the limiting that "you need money to make money" hold you back.

You may need to start small to work your way up. Maybe you wish to start a new healthy fast food business, entirely vegan friendly. As we said before, you need to focus on years rather than days. Start small, maybe start through making vegan snacks to sell to your local community, or drafting an eBook about how to cook your favourite meals as a vegan. Work your way up from here – as you climb higher you will be able to achieve more and money will come, it really will. The key, though, is not to do it for the money, do it for the dream. Do it for yourself.

STARTING A BUSINESS WITHOUT MONEY

While mindset and mentality is absolutely key to creating a successful business without money, you're probably wondering how exactly do you go about doing so.

Below are a number of different starting points for you to begin with.

1. CREATING

If you have any level of skill in arts and crafts, creating things to sell can be a great place to start. Although gathering materials in order to create may involve some costs, these products can then be sold for far more than they cost to make. Many huge companies started out through simply making things to sell.

The best places online to sell your products easily are Etsy, Abe's Market, Bonanza and eBay. These sites can also be a great place to search for ideas and inspiration.

2. RESELLING

If you're not the artsy type and don't have space to store products, reselling can be a great way to earn money as a retailer rather than a manufacturer.

Dropshipping is a great way to earn money through resales. Dropshipping is the process of advertising a product that you do not own. When this product is purchased, you place an order from a wholesaler and have the product shipped directly to the customer. This way, you never actually handle the product but still make a profit through selling it at a higher price than it is purchased at.

Browsing thrift stores and antique shops can also be a great way to find products to resell at a higher price. Oftentimes, shops of this nature stock items that they know little about and thus do not sell them as highly as they could. You, a reseller, can take full advantage of this.

3. MAXIMISING YOUR EXPERTISE

Another great way to earn money is to sell your services. If you are skilled in a particular area, say, mechanics or playing a musical instrument (or speaking English, French, writing poetry – anything you can do well) then you could sell these skills to other people. This way, you can earn through teaching somebody to do something you love doing anyway. Selling your services requires no startup costs and could lead to developing a successful business further down the line. Even if a business is not started, this can be a great way to earn some cash to help you start your business.

It's clear to see that the belief that "you need money to make money" is a common misconception. There are a wealth of methods to not only starting your business but earning money to fund it without having to put any in. Take each of these methods and make them your own. Find what works best for you and the money will come.

CHAPTER 10.

WEALTH CONSCIOUSNESS.

Wealth consciousness is an incredibly powerful tool for increasing your riches…

…Consciousness in itself is an awareness of something. If you are conscious, you are aware of your surroundings; if you are self-conscious, you are aware of yourself and likely focussing your attention on your image. If you are *wealth* conscious, you are aware of your wealth.

People that are wealth conscious are not so just because they are wealthy. Being conscious of your wealth does not require any sum of money, moreover it determines how a person will regard their financial losses and gains. A person that is wealth conscious likely will not go extended periods having very little money as they are aware of their income and outcome and will manage their spending. Wealth consciousness is a mindset that acts as a magnet, a way of thinking that will ensure a person remains financially stable at all times.

Being conscious and being mindful are often considered the same thing, and this assumption is fair. Mindfulness is a state of being that ignores the past and the future and focuses on the here and now. In reality, the present is the only moment that truly exists because both the past and and the future are fleeting and yet to be experienced.

WEALTH CONSCIOUSNESS & MEDITATION

Meditation is the practice of bringing the attention to the present moment and is key to becoming wealth conscious for it enables us to live fully in the here and now. There are a whole load of meditation practices around, some focusing on the breath as a tool to direct the attention to the present, others using physical movements such as yoga. Find which practice suits you and dedicate a small (or large, depending on your availability) time slot each day to it – whether it be twenty minutes, ten, five (there are even *one* minute meditation methods out there!) – every little really does help.

To give you a brief overview of the practice of meditation, I will outline a method I use and have found to be successful in reducing anxiety and boosting mindfulness.

1. Find a comfortable, seated position in which you will not be disturbed.

2. Close your eyes and take deep breaths, breathing into your stomach/abdomen rather than the chest.

3. With every in-breath, count one, and two with every out-breath. Focus your attention entirely on your breath, feeling the sensations over your body as the breath enters and exists. You may find it easiest to focus on the tingles around the nostrils as the breath moves through them, or to focus on the inflation of the stomach with every inhale. Whatever works for you – there is not right or

wrong method.

4. Try to dismiss any thoughts that come to mind. There will be many, this is okay. Try not to judge your thoughts, marking them as unhelpful or bad, or even positive. Just allow them to float freely over you and recognise them as being separate from you – you are not your thoughts.

5. Continue this practice for as long as you wish. There is no time limit. I try to meditate for at least ten minutes a day and find that to be just right. Find what works for you.

6. Repeat. Repetition is key and if you do not intend to meditate daily then I wouldn't recommend meditating at all. Thoughts may fly straight away, 'I don't have time for this', 'I have so much work to do and I'm sat here thinking about breathing'. **These are just thoughts, they are not you**. Think of yourself as a mountain. Clouds may pass over you, but they are not you. Your thoughts are the clouds.

How To Boost Your Wealth Consciousness

1. An important step to take is to quit avoiding money, brushing it under the carpet and acting as though your payments are being made from some invisible source that replenishes itself. Look your money in it's eyes for what it is. You are not bound by your income, it does not control you and you should not

fear it – just be conscious of it. Keep a track of your earnings and losses and don't be afraid to check your bank balance. I would recommend opening a spreadsheet (I use Google Sheets) to keep a loose track of your financial developments. In doing this, you can increase your income steadily simply by controlling and being aware of your transactions.

2. Have a conversation with your future, financially stable self. How have they got to this place? What attitudes have they had towards money to get there? Create that reality.

3. Do not feel guilty about making money. The premise that a rich man cannot enter the gates of heaven is simply a myth. While yes, giving to charities and spending on others is essential – it is essential for personal growth and happiness and keeping balance in the world, you should not feel guilty for earning money and saving money. There are many ways of giving, spending money is certainly a less significant way than, say, giving love and support to others. If you wish to be charitable then give gifts richer than wealth and do not feel guilty for earning money.

4. Wealth that has not been earned will not stay. If money was simply given to you, let's say you won a million on the lottery, you would not have developed the intelligence to keep hold of it. The process of earning money through putting in effort develops your values for it and, in turn, your ability

to sustain it. Hard work is important in any field, including earning money. There is a difference, though, between hard work and worthwhile work. While you may slave 56 weekly hours at a full-time job, you are not maximising your earning potential. Work of this nature does not encourage personal growth. Working smart, however, will initiate a positive multiplier effect that will increase your profit overtime.

For more on working smart through establishing multiple revenue streams, click here.

CAN I ASK A FAVOUR?

If you enjoyed this book, found it useful or otherwise then I'd really appreciate it if you would post a short review on Amazon.

I do read all the reviews personally so that I can continually write about what people are interested in.

Thanks for your support!

Julian Goldie